How to Live in the
MILLENNIUM

Gina Welsh

Library of Congress Control Number: 2023920000
Paperback: 979-8-9886071-9-9

Contents

Forward to the Foreword

As you read through this little book, you may notice some repetition. Yes, I repeat a few things. Why? Well, repetition is one of the most effective ways to learn. And since we have entered a new age, a new world on God's timetable, some things bear repeating. Reminders as you go along. Bringing to remembrance. Wash, rinse, repeat.

So, I ask that you just put up with it and read to the end.

FOREWORD

We have entered a new age. A new world. The Millennium. Are you surprised? Didn't you think that we would get there? I mean, just about everything else God said has come to pass. And now, too, so has this Age of Shalom. But now what?

All of the teachings of Jesus still apply. Even more so. There is nothing new under the sun except for one very big and glaring thing – Satan is off planet! And his minions! He is not here anymore. He does not have reign on earth anymore. He is bound and rendered completely powerless – more than that. He is ABSENT! MIA! GONE! This was foretold. Read it! In Revelation 20: (NKJV)

[1] And I saw an angel come down from heaven, having the key of the bottomless pit and a great chain in his hand.

[2] And he laid hold on the dragon, that old serpent, which is the Devil, and Satan, and bound him a thousand years,

[3] And cast him into the bottomless pit, and shut him up, and set a seal upon him, that he should deceive the nations no more, till the thousand years should be fulfilled: and after that he must be loosed a little season.

So now what? Read through the scriptures again, particularly the New Testament, and take Satan out of the equation. We no longer have to battle with, stand against, resist him. We have ourselves now to deal with. And us firsties – we who are in the very beginning of the Millennial reign, will have the most difficult time because we still have in our memories, almost our DNA, strong associations with Satan and all he has stood for and done for thousands of years.

Now, instead of rebuking him, we must correct ourselves. Now instead of blaming him, we must take accountability for ourselves. Not through condemnation – that's the old way! But through this new age of Shalom! Satan is not here anymore to lie to us, whisper in our ears, oppress or possess, trick, constantly hassle us and get in our way! Now we are free to finally grow up, grow beautiful, grow strong, overcome without objections, really be ourselves.

Let's begin....

CHAPTER 1

No Longer

We are no longer in the "end times." We are in the Millennium. At the very beginning, but IN it. We are not still waiting for Satan to be bound. He IS bound right now. He has been bound since 2012.

I was born into the end times in 1962. I was born a Christian. Baptized at age 6. Received the gift of the Holy Ghost with evidence of speaking in tongues at the age of 9. Shortly thereafter, at 9, I was prophesized over and received my calling to be a Leader. I have known since I was 9 years old that I would see the return of our Lord Jesus Christ. Not for us – the Church. But for the Jews.

In late November 1983, I and many of my fellow Brothers and Sisters in the Lord attended the Marriage Supper of the Lamb. Physical banquets held in churches here on earth reflected the heavenly supper. Six years later I experienced the "Rapture." A very powerful and strong experience. (That word "Rapture" is not in the bible, by the way, but the Church sure likes to use it a lot.) A couple of years or so after that I received my first crown. The

Crown of Life. Several years after that I received my second crown – The Crown of Glory. Upon study of the scriptures I knew that the third crown, The Crown of Righteousness was to be given out to many, many, many people at the same time. That happened in the early part of the year 2015.

In late Spring/early Summer of 2015, God commissioned me to remove all the demons that had been left here on earth after Satan was removed and bound – for 1,000 years. I had had experiences with demons off and on over the years – so I guess I was long equipped and prepared. I was not the only one God commissioned to do this. He had people all over the world doing this same work at the same time. The first demon I ran into physically jerked the poor woman he was possessing into my path and leered at me! He knew what I was about to do. It only took a couple of months. But the demons have all been rounded up and put into "nursery" as I call it. They have to stay there for the duration of the Millennium.

So why this huge stinking mess the world is in? Hmmm? Satan has been ruling on this earth for so long, spreading his lies, whispering in our ears, that his way of doing things is almost, *almost,* in our very DNA. Before he was caught and bound, he came through the earth like a HUGE tsunami. What is left in the wake of a huge tsunami? Utter destruction. Then decay. Stink. Disease. Putrefaction.

Then, slowly but surely, the land heals. Things start to grow back – even better because new silt and earth has been left behind, fertilized by the decay. Rebuilding takes place.

We are not still waiting for all the horrible predictions of the Bible to come to pass. Most of them already have. However, at the time of this writing, there are some left that must yet come to pass in order to cleanse the earth and allow this new Millennial Age to blossom into fullness. But be not afraid!

I could go on and on. But I will keep it to this. We are in the Millennium. God told me to not wait for the rest of my Brothers and Sisters in Christ to get it. But I am to start living each day as if I am in the Millennium, because I am. We all are. It is time to step into Peace and start cleaning and rebuilding.

We, the Church, already have Jesus. It is the Jews' time now.

Praise God! Thank you Jesus!

CHAPTER 2

The Tribulation

I was watching/listening to Pastor Creflo Dollar on the internet on a Saturday morning in June 2016. The subject everyone is in agreement about in recent weeks is Faith. Good stuff! However, all of the Pastors that have been within my earshot, and including the ones younger than myself (I am almost 54 years old at the time of this writing) are still preaching that Satan is alive and well on the earth and we are in the end times. NO! He ain't here – Satan is not here anymore! He hasn't been since 2012! And neither are his multitudes of demons and demonic forces! I know! I was given the duty of ridding them in the Spring and Summer of 2015. (Me and, I feel certain, a number of people around the world – as I stated in the previous chapter.) The pastors have also been talking about laws – laws of heaven, laws of Christ, laws of sin and death, etc. and our legal authority here in the earth. That in order for God to do a work, any work, in the earth, we, as the legal 'owners' of the earth must 'allow' it, make provision for it, call it in, give permission.

As I was contemplating these things while listening to Pastor Dollar, the Lord told me to go fetch the book "The Greatest Book on Dispensational

Truth in the World" by Clarence Larkin, copyrighted in 1918. I hadn't thought about this book in a while. A very valuable book. I fetched the book and quickly landed on the page right after page 19 which has the chart titled "The Relation of Jew, Gentile and Church to Each Other."

Now I have known for a couple of years now that we are in the Millennium. Not the end times that everyone insists on hanging onto. We are at the beginning of the Millennium – but in it we are! Satan has been bound since the year 2012. The demons have been cast into what I call 'nursery' since 2015. So how does this reconcile? I have been taught my whole life that we are waiting for the 'rapture' (which, by the way, is not a word used anywhere in the bible) but refers to the catching out of the church before The Tribulation. As if the tribulation was for all the inhabitants of the earth. I have been waiting for this all my life – as I have been taught by the preachers and teachers over the years. They are still teaching this. NO! Not so! I looked at the chart and noticed that the Jews are depicted, starting with Abraham, as a flow through to the Millennial Kingdom. It flows from Abraham, to Jesus on the Cross, to the Church, to the catching out of the Church, to the Tribulation, Judgment of Nations and then the Millennial Kingdom. The Tribulation! OMG! It is not the whole world that goes thru the Tribulation! It certainly isn't the Church that goes thru it! It's the Jews and they alone!

Then the Lord instructed me to look up the dates of WWII. WWII was from 1939 – 1945. WWII was in each of seven years. And what happened to the Jews during WWII? The Tribulation! See it? The Church is considered caught out because it was not part of the Tribulation in the first place! The Tribulation was for the Jews! It ended in 1945. I was born in 1962. AFTER the Tribulation. Praise God! We are still waiting for something that has already happened and is completed!

It is time for us all to understand where we are now in history and prophecy and to start living as if we are in the Millennium because we are!

Jesus' second coming is not for the Church but for the Jews! Our (The Church) Jesus is here with us now. Jeshua, coming back for the Jews, is coming soon – in fact may very well already be here. I would not be the least bit surprised if He wasn't already here. The Jews have all been gathered back to Israel.

I have known since I was a little girl, that I would see the fulfillment of the scriptures and the return of the Lord. It is here. Now. We are not waiting to get through the end times. They were the bulk of the 20ᵗʰ Century. I was born into the end of the end times. New flash! Just because we insist on hanging onto the end times, does not make it so! God's timing is His timing. So let's get on board with God! It's time.

It is time to move Forward!

CHAPTER 3

Door to Heaven

Early in June of 2016 on a Friday evening, I was talking on the phone with my little brother. We were discussing a visitation he had had just recently from Jesus, who told him that the door to heaven was so close that it was 'right there.' For some reason, that struck a deep chord in me. I let that settle into my spirit.

The next morning I got up and did my usual. Grabbed my bibles and went on line to listen to some teaching or preaching. I usually listen to KCM, but sometimes Creflo Dollar, Keith Moore, Jessie DuPlantis, etc. I believe that this particular morning I was again listening to Brother Dollar. When I suddenly got up and start praising the Lord and pacing between the living room and dining room. Then a door appeared in the middle of the living room (where there is no door) and without hesitation I walked through the door. I was suddenly on a cliff overlooking a huge valley. There were snow covered mountains all around. The sky was as blue as I ever hope to see. The air was absolutely clear, crisp, pristine. It was so beautiful and I knew that I was in heaven. Earth has some stunningly beautiful places and I have had the privilege to witness a couple of them, but nothing like this!

Then I looked about me and I saw that there were multitudes of people with me, we were all on horses. We were clothed in light so that all you could see was luminous white. I had a sense that we wore armor of light. I looked to my left and there was Jesus on his horse. He and I and a line of others were at the edge of the cliff looking out over the vast valley. Stretching back behind us, to the left, to the right and straight back as far as you could see were the multitudes dress in light upon horses. Then I opened my mouth and raised my arms and sounded off a long note as loud as I could. I waved my arm up to the right and the people sounded off. I waved my arm up to the left and the people there sounded off. I turned in my saddle and lifted my arm behind and they sounded off. A battle cry of victory? A victory cry of battle? I was deeply affected. It stayed with me all day – that sense that I was in heaven.

We are ready. It is time. The move is on.

CHAPTER 4

Lucifer

When I was 20 years old, newly married, my then husband and I had a brief sojourn in a small apartment in Lacey, WA. I was in between jobs for a few days. One day I was alone in the living room and I felt a terrible and dreadful presence in the room. I turned and looked and standing in the doorway of the bedroom that was just off the living room was Lucifer. Yes, THE Lucifer. He filled the doorway. He was the most beautiful 'man' I had ever seen. Exquisitely beautiful! Words cannot adequately describe! I have not seen before or since such a beautiful creature. And I am positive that I was not seeing him in his full glory but rather through shadow. I have never felt such fear as that. Not before or since. I was terrified! He stood there looking at me with a smile on his face. Just looking at me. I wanted desperately to flee the apartment, but either I refused to let the fear make me run or I couldn't run for some reason I know not. Which, I am not sure. I told him to leave in the Name of Jesus, but he did not. He stood there looking at me for what seemed a long time but wasn't more than few minutes. Then he was gone. And I could breathe again.

Then the next day he came back. I was alone. He stood in the same doorway, watching me with that same smile on his face, for several minutes. Oh the beauty! Oh the terror! Telling him to leave in Jesus' Name had no effect. He left when he was ready to leave.

Then the third day. Again. Oh Lord why is he doing this?? He came. Stood. Watched. Smiled. And then finally left.

I have not seen him since.

I had many strange and perhaps even dangerous experiences during the year I was 20 years old. If Hollywood were to get my story, with some embellishing, they could make one heck of a horror movie out of it! But of all the experiences that year, Lucifer's visit was, by far, the most deeply affecting. And compelling.

And, I think it is connected to why now I am being called by God to write a book about How To Live In The Millennium.

CHAPTER 5

Creation Vibration

God is a Creator. He loves creating! And my oh my! He is very good at it! And he super-duper likes it when he has co-creators or is a co-creator. Unlike the angels, we are not creations of God, but we are God. Okay, if it makes you feel better, we are children of God. God spun around and sparks streamed off. We are those sparks. Each one of us is a piece of God.

Faith is a creation process. It starts with a thought. Nothing can happen unless you first think it. No thought. No creation. A songwriter must first have a thought on what the first line or first word of a song will be. The painter – what the first stroke of the brush should be. The architect. The chef. The inventor. The teacher. The person who wants to make a difference in their community. You.

The thought must then be spoken out loud. Sound is a vibration. Speaking a specific thought out loud produces specific vibrations that travel through the air. Since space is not empty, when the sound vibrations travel through space it pushes, rearranges the space around the vibration which in turns moves and rearranges outward – like the concentric circles of waves the radiate outward when a stone is dropped into a body of water.

Now here's an important feature to know. The spoken thoughts are processed through 'laws' of the universe. As God is Love and Good and has given us the parameters in which to couch our thoughts through the law of love: Philippians 4:8 *AMPC* For the rest, brethren, whatever is true, whatever is worthy of reverence and is honorable and seemly, whatever is just, whatever is pure, whatever is lovely and lovable, whatever is kind and winsome and gracious, if there is any virtue and excellence, if there is anything worthy of praise, think on and weigh and take account of these things [fix your minds on them]; then when a thought is released through spoken vibrations, it ascends much like a plane in takeoff ascends up into the heavenlies which then continues on until it reaches its designed destination.

Conversely, when a thought comes under the law of sin and death and is released through spoken vibration, it is like a rock being thrown. It does not fly or soar but rather lashes out, falls and hits the ground. The impact of which is damaging, displacing, tearing, rending.

So, as God created with the spoken word. We create with our spoken words. After the word(s) are spoken, then an action must take place. So roll up your sleeves, cause here we go!

CHAPTER 6

The Parts of Us

Most of us, perhaps not all, but most of us have different parts to us. Potential split personalities, if you will.

A few years ago I 'saw' my personalities. Seven of them to be exact. Of course, the one that stuck out to me the most was the 'dark one'. She/He is cool, sleek, very black and very smooth. Takes no prisoners. The one who could walk up and blow your brains out with a pistol, whisper the smoke from the barrel, put the pistol in He/She's pocket, and with a smile turn around and saunter away. The one who takes no crap. The one were testosterone lives. The one who could probably hang with the devil and his gang, except that She/He finds them unworthy of She/He's company. She/He finds the devil and his gang nonsensical and of low repute. My first and old school taught reaction was to rebuke and cast out this dark entity. She/He would rise up inside me when my husband was being a jerk. (Sorry Darlin, but sometimes…. what can I say?) And had I been a man, She/He would have been given permission to do some 'correcting.' So She/He is evil, right? The dark side of me. So get out in the name of Jesus I say! Guess what? She/He went nowhere. Hmpff! So, in my mind's eye, I told She/He to shut up. Sit over in that corner and don't say a word. I put a rather handsome purple hat on She/He's head, which I thought looked rather fetching on Him/Her. (Ah look, how maternal of me!) She/He, with great patience, did as I commanded. Sat in the corner and shut up.

Then I noticed the others. Some shorter, some taller. Some female, some male. One girl has on an old fashioned dress, soft brown with tiny pale yellow flowers on it. The rest of them, for the most part, are non-descript. Don't stand out like She/He. Perhaps because they are softer, gentler, non-confrontational. The girl in the dress is definitely a child. About 6 or 7 years old. As I pondered them, I got the sense that if I did not address this 'issue,' one or more of them could 'split' off into their own separate self and thus apart from me. Well, this is NOT acceptable! So I turned around and told all of them – and yes, with much trepidation, this includes She/He – that we are to gather together as one. We are one. ONE not seven different – but all together as one. That there will be no splitting off. No making of spiritual babies, if you will. (More on that some other time, perhaps, if God wills.) Rather like a hen gathering her chicks under her wings. So, those seven plus me makes eight as one. Me is the embodiment of them.

So what about the dark one? Yes, what about She/He? It took a little bit but I finally started to realize that She/He is the strength of me. The balance to my softer, weaker self. The one, if I utilize Him/Her's truth, that lends me the fortitude to get things done. To stand strong. The rod in my spine.

Of course, if I were to let this one rule my life, it could get pretty ugly. And as we all have the potential for evil, She/He would be the ruler of this if I did not have the Lord Jesus and the Word of God to submit all of me to. For the past several thousand years we have had Satan and his minions constantly whispering in our ears, talking especially to the most receptive parts of us. We have had to armor ourselves, stand on the Word of God, constantly resist the devil at every turn. Satan has even convinced some of us that it is that dark part of us that he's after when really it is the little girl in the brown flowered dress..... hmmmm?

But Satan is no longer here. Neither are his minions. So, we are left with ourselves. Now the evil is ours. We get to no longer point fingers and say "the devil made me do it!" We can no longer blame Satan for tempting us, whispering in our ears. Now we must own up to our own selves. And the darkness that is potential in each of us, as it has always been, is still there. Now we can start to really hear our own selves without the distraction of Satan and his minions. Peace.

For me, personally, I no longer see She/He as a dark and potentially evil being (which is a very real possibility). But as a strength that can be used to stand strong in who I am. And as long as all of me stands in the truth of the two great commandments: I shall love the Lord my God with all my heart, soul, mind and strength; And I shall love my neighbor as myself, we now are ready to walk in peace in this Millennium. And create!

It bears repeating: Philippians 4:8, *AMPC* – For the rest, brethren, whatever is true, whatever is worthy of reverence and is honorable and seemly, whatever is just, whatever is pure, whatever is lovely and lovable, whatever is kind and winsome and gracious, if there is any virtue and excellence, if there is anything worthy of praise, think on and weigh and take account of these things [fix your minds on them].

I particularly like the word "winsome" which means: generally pleasing and engaging often because of a childlike charm and innocence.

Let us walk in peace. Let us begin.

CHAPTER 7

Anarchy

The Hidden Man of the Heart. As the physical heart is the blood pump, so the hidden man of the heart is the spiritual blood pump. And the blood is the Blood of the New Covenant.

Why, you may ask, if Satan and his minions are gone, have we, the world gone into such disarray and violence?

Because Satan, too, had a government – a legal system through which his every operation was conducted. Law is law is law. As there is earthy and universal laws such as gravity. And laws that work in cahoots with other laws such as the law of lift of an airplane which supersedes the law of gravity. However, the law of lift still works in tandem with the law of gravity, else an airplane would fly off the planet into space with little to no effort. Checks and balances and laws that interact with other laws.

There are laws of the spirit. Law of Faith = God. Law of Fear = Satan. Life through the Law of Christ. Death through the law of sin and condemnation.

Even Satan himself, fallen though he is, must operate through a form of government, perverse though it may be, because all in all is governed by laws.

So then, all the peoples of the earth who have been ruled and operating under the government of Satan, now have no governmental authority. It has become anarchy. And as much as we might love the concept of a 'utopian' society (see definition of utopian below), history has shown that left utterly on our own without some form of government, we decay into utter destruction which then goes into ending.

Definition of UTOPIAN
1. **1:** of, relating to, or having the characteristics of a utopia; *especially* : having impossibly ideal conditions especially of social organization
2. **2:** proposing or advocating impractically ideal social and political schemes *<utopianidealists>*
3. **3:** impossibly ideal : visionary *<recognised the utopian nature of his hopes — C. S. Kilby>*
4. **4:** believing in, advocating, or having the characteristics of utopian socialism *<utopiandoctrines>* *<utopian novels>* - **Merriam-Webster Dictionary**

In other words, they are running around with no leadership, no governance, no direction, selfish without training, blindly making decisions not taking into account the laws of both spirit and flesh. Perversion. Destruction. Love cannot function here.

This is a good time then to kick 'religion' all the way to the curb. And usher in the Love and Peace of God through the government of Jesus Christ our Lord. It is time to roll up our sleeves and do the work of Love and Peace. Of restoring our planet. Of shining the light of love, forgiveness, without judgment. Of genuinely and fully loving God with all our hearts, minds, souls and might and really REALLY knowing what it is to love our neighbor as ourselves. It is time for us to fully realize that we really can no longer accuse the accuser and let that be the excuse to continue with something that is now in the past.

As I heard a Native American brother say just this morning: "Always go forward, never look back." It is time to go forward and learn to walk in this, the Millennium, sans Satan and his minions. It is time to walk in peace. And it is time to take technology to the next level(s).

Go and help those that you can. Show them the way out of anarchy if they are willing. Let the shalom come. Let it come. And do your part.

CHAPTER 8

THE POWER OF "SHUT UP"!!!

Shut up! Shut up! Shut up your mouths! Clamp them shut! Do NOT say what you are thinking! Not until you have cleaned up your thinking! Don't even mutter it under your breath! Especially don't mutter under your breath! Do you think that by muttering it won't be heard? Do you think the whisper moves the atmosphere any less than speaking or shouting?

Don't you realize that if God, with the slightest, almost imperceptible flick of his pinky finger can cause all the angels that are flying around his throne in the throne room to violently fling into the farthest wall, what can we do with our spoken words? We little g's.?

God's spoken word created the entire universe. Each one of our spoken words create a change in the room, in the community, in the city, in the country, in the world, in the solar system. And the only reason we haven't spoken ourselves into complete chaos and annihilation is because there have always been people speaking words of creation, of love, of forgiveness, of beauty, of grace, of mercy, of kindness, of respect – to counter words of anger, destruction, chaos. And just think, if these words of grace didn't have to counter words of death, what would our planet be like? If these words of grace were released sans blockage?

Now think what this world will be like if we SHUT UP! Clean up our thoughts. Take the time to silence our mouths and train out of ourselves the thousands of years (at the very least) of Satan's rule, his murmurings and whisperings in our ears, coming out of our mouths, leading us to feel justified to say what we want when we want no matter how hurtful or destructive. Tit for tat. Petulance. Tantrums. "J-U-S-T-I-F-I-C-A-T-I-O-N."

This is not political correctness! This is not suppressing our freedom of speech! Ha! The Devil has had fun bullying us with those! This is getting his garbage out of our very DNA, out of our ears, out of our thoughts. It's evolution. It is time for the next evolution! A world without Satan and his minions? Our old ways do not apply. WE must learn how to live in the world now without Satan and his minions.

And since I am writing to we Christians, and the government is now on the shoulders of Jesus Christ in rule of this earth, we must be His leaders in this! It starts with us in earnest to SHUT UP! Be honest. Stop and think about the times your mutter under your breath about your husband or wife or children or boss. Or speak out against the news or a politician or world leader. Or or or??? How unaware are we that we're doing it daily? SHUT UP!

How are we to get to the year 2525 (hear that song in your head?) and have it not be like that song? We must start now, at the beginning of this thousand year Shalom. And it MUST start with our words! We must be angry and not curse (and no I don't mean cuss words although that too). To curse is to decrease – to curse someone is to cause them some form of decrease. How would you like someone to contribute to decreasing in your life by the words they speak to you? Or behind your back? And yes, this is a lesson I am still working on myself.

Galatians 5: 22-23

22 But the fruit of the Spirit is love, joy, peace, longsuffering, gentleness, goodness, faith,

23 Meekness, temperance: against such there is no law.

James 3: 10 Out of the same mouth proceed blessing and cursing. My brethren, these things ought not to be so.

11 Does a spring send forth fresh water and bitter from the same opening?

12 Can a fig tree, my brethren, bear olives, or a grapevine bear figs? Thus no spring yields both salt water and fresh

So utilized The Power of "Shut Up"! To stop and rethink, retrain our thoughts and then speak words of life, love, healing, patience, kindness, wisdom, faith to everyone and every situation.

Besides, we have a <u>mere</u> 1,000 years before Satan and his minions are released to come and try us again. We need to be soooooo ready that he will flop BIG time because we have matured so much that our words of creation and blessing will cause his words to fall flat and decrease into nothing.

Just imagine. Not fluffy unrealistic utopian perfection – but a peaceful world where all the peoples of the earth can live quiet, Godly and peaceable lives. Where we can actually go out and visit other stars and planets because earth is a safe haven. We have ended all wars and conflicts, and stopped inflicting pain and so called justice – of the eye for an eye variety on our fellow Earthlings. That we can steward the planet as we were meant to in the original Garden of Eden.

The time is NOW. Let's clean up our DNA and speak only words of Life! And we start this by Shutting UP!

CHAPTER 9

_____ **Christ**

Go grab a pencil. Better yet, a pen. Go on, we can wait.

Now, write your first name on the line above. Yes. On the line above right next to "Christ".

CHAPTER 10

Satan's Gone. Now What?

Yes, we are still being told that we are in the last days, and by the current looks of things, you would think that is true! My my but it seems as if we have all lost our blooming minds! So much hatred! So much judgment! Murders and racism escalation! Terrorism! Justifications! What the ???

But we are no longer in the last days. We are in the Millennium. So what gives? Why all the increase in behaviors that we should be past now? Why the uptick in the above mentions?

Anarchy. Satan and his minions are MIA. Believe it that Satan had a very distinct governmental system. A system of hierarchies. There was a certain order to things. An answering to the next higher up. Orders given and carried out. Now that he and the rest of his crew are gone, there is a HUGE void on the earth where his governmental system use to be. And we humans really are not equipped to be left to our own devices – so to speak. We need leadership. Governing. Rules and order. Direction. Otherwise, and this is scientific as well, "all hell breaks loose" and we descend into chaos. All the people who were operating their lives under Satan's government, and there are a LOT of those people out there, are now in anarchy. They have no ruler. No governance. Oy vey! What a mess!

So, it is up to us, those who are under the government of God through our Lord Jesus Christ, to step up and spread the mantle. The mantle of the government of Shalom. Of Peace. Be the shining example. Keep close watch on every single word that proceeds out of your mouth at ALL times. Speak Shalom. Work in Shalom. Roll up your sleeves and work in Shalom. SHOW everyone around you by the words of your mouth and your following actions how to live, work, play in Shalom. Stay in Love. Stay in Peace. Every moment of every day, everywhere you go.

And don't judge!!!!! Don't condemn!!!! Be strong. Be courageous. Be busy working, planning, building, growing, fixing, adding, changing, LIVING in Shalom! Show them by your words and actions! Place your hand on their shoulder and with love, accept them, give understanding and respect to them, and then show them the Shalom. How they, on an individual level, have and can enter a state of "completeness, soundness, welfare, peace." See below:

Question: "What is the meaning of the Hebrew word *shalom*?"

Answer: Commonly translated as "peace" and used as both a greeting and farewell, *shalom* has rich meaning in Hebrew. "Peace" is an accurate translation of the term, but *shalom* implies more than lack of conflict. According to Strong's Exhaustive Concordance, *shalom* means "completeness, soundness, welfare, peace." It is translated "success" and used as part of an inspired blessing in 1 Chronicles 12:18. *Shalom* is applicable to an external peace between two entities—such as individuals or nations—and to an internal sense of peace within the individual.

The ESV and NRSV title Isaiah 54 "The Eternal Covenant of Peace." In part, God promises, "'Though the mountains be shaken and the hills be removed, yet my unfailing love for you will not be shaken nor my covenant of peace be removed' says the Lord, who has compassion on you. . . . All your children will be taught by the Lord, and great will be their peace" (Isaiah 54:10, 13). One of the names of God is Yahweh-Shalom (Judges 6:24), or the Lord our Peace. Jesus is called the Prince of Peace (Isaiah 9:6). ~ gotquestions.org/shalom-meaning.html

Show them how to truly love their neighbor as themselves. That each of us wants love, acceptance. To receive that love and acceptance of ourselves and to give that same allowance to others. Shalom! Don't teach them. SHOW them!

Step up people! The time is NOW!

CHAPTER 11

A Practical Example of Faith

James 1:22 King James Version (KJV)

²² But be ye doers of the word, and not hearers only, deceiving your own selves.

I was addicted to and smoked cigarettes for 13 years. I did NOT want to be a smoker. I did NOT like being addicted to cigarettes. I prayed for deliverance for all of those 13 years. I prayed over and over that I would quit. Sometimes, it seemed that it was impossible! I'd been praying and praying and the years rolled by with no changes. But I didn't give up. I kept praying.

The first few years I would go through self-condemnation. I'd pray for deliverance from smoking and feel bad that I hadn't quit yet! A vicious little cycle.

Then one day, it occurred to me that I needed to kick the self-condemnation to the curb! That was not helping one bit! Perhaps even interfering, counteracting, my words of prayer and supplication. So I stopped condemning myself. I stopped judging myself as smoker who didn't want to be a smoker but couldn't seem to kick the habit by myself. I allowed myself to be a smoker free of the condemnation and judgment. I smoke. So what? I love myself. I will keep praying and professing that I am free from the additions of nicotine and smoking. Petitioning God for my deliverance from something that I genuinely did not want in my life.

And the years went by. And I would wake up in the morning hacking and coughing so hard that I thought I might spew my very lungs out. Then light up another cigarette. Because I was addicted.

Then, one morning, after 13 years, I woke up coughing and hacking. I had come down with a chest cold so the coughing and hacking was worse than normal. But, I 'needed' a cigarette. I lit a cigarette. Took one puff. Starting coughing. Then I heard the Lord say to me "You will never smoke another cigarette again from this moment forward." Yeah? Really? And then the absolute revelation, knowing, certainty hit me! Yes!! YES!!!!!!!!!!!!! I am never going to smoke another cigarette again as long as I live!!!!! Hallelujah!!!! Woot Woot! Thank you God! Thank you Jesus!!!! It was finished! I finally had my break through! My deliverance! And it was as sure in my heart and my head as it ever was going to be! So I crushed the pack of cigarettes and threw them away with a big grin on my face, *knowing* I would never smoke another cigarette.

Now here's the doing part of the Word. The doing part of Faith. My mind was released from the addiction of the cigarettes. Fully. I would, very easily, with no effort at all, ever smoke, ever desire to smoke another cigarette again. And I haven't either! (At the time of this writing I have not smoke in 14 years.) But my body was still addicted. The withdrawals for me was extreme tiredness, lethargy and the absolute inability to concentrate on anything.

So, I got the patch. And I slowly over the next 8 weeks weaned my body off nicotine. Starting at full strength and slowing reducing how much nicotine my body was receiving. When I had it at the lowest dose at the end of the eight week, I finally had to take the patch off. I still had to go through 3 more days of withdrawal – which consisted mostly of being tired. But then I was finally free in my body as well. My body now lined up with my mind, and my spirit.

See?

CHAPTER 12

Some Personal History

I was born a Christian. Yes really! But it didn't become a consciousness for me until I was five years old.

When I was six years old, I asked to be baptized. We were living in Woodlake, California, at the time. I asked old Pastor Leak of the little Pentecostal Church there to baptize me. He was in his 70s at that time – so pretty old considering I was only 6. He baptized me in a cow trough on one of the parishioner's country home property. Full immersion. I remember being very happy when I came back out of the water. And my immediate next thing to accomplish? Receiving the infilling of the Holy Ghost!

So I started praying for the Holy Ghost to come fill me. But Satan immediately started taunting me that I would never receive the Holy Ghost! I am six years old and I am already doing battle with Satan! I went to old Pastor Leak after church service one Sunday (I am still 6 years old) and told him that Satan was telling me that I would never get the Holy Ghost and would Pastor pray for me? He did right on the spot.

So I continued praying and turn seven. Then eight. Still praying. Still not having received. I remember when I was eight, we were living in apartment above an auto, electric, etc. parts warehouse in the downtown warehouse district of Portland, Oregon, at that time. Satan came to me in a dream, again taunting me and telling me that I will NEVER get the Holy Ghost! I will too! I will too! I yelled in my dream. I have not forgotten that dream. It was upsetting and made me more determined than ever to get the Holy Ghost!

Still, I kept praying and asking for the Holy Ghost to come into me. I remember going down to the front of the church during altar calls, praying and asking God to send me the Holy Ghost. People would lay hands on me and pray for me to receive the Holy Ghost. Nothing.

Another year goes by. It is summer and I have just turned 9 years old. We are now living in a large apartment complex in the St. John district of Portland, Oregon. There were several buildings in the complex. Each building housed four apartments. In an apartment building over to our left lived the Snows. In apartment building over to our right, lived the Wilsons. These were members of our Church. The Wilsons had a daughter my age. The Snow's kids were a bit younger but Rebecca Snow was a good friend of my Mama's.

One day, Mama and us kids were over visiting the Snows when Brother Wilson comes in all excited! His daughter (same age as me) just received the indwelling of the Holy Ghost! The adults all started rejoicing and praising God! Me? I got PISSED OFF!!!!!! I went into the bathroom and closed the door. I was ANGRY! And I let God know it! I had been trying for three years to get the indwelling of the Holy Ghost! And then Brother Wilson, who I really didn't like very much at all, comes in gushing about how his daughter just received the Holy Ghost. And she's my age! I told God "I want the Holy Ghost and I want it NOW!"

I suspect God was trying not to laugh too hard at me! This little 9 year old yelling at Him! Angry with Him!

I left the bathroom and went into the living room where the adults were. They took one look at me and knew something was wrong. They asked me and I told them! I want the Holy Ghost! I've been praying for years! And the next thing I know, I was speaking in other tongues!

Needless to say, there was even more rejoicing going on in that little apartment!

Sometimes..... sometimes.... you just got to get angry!!!

CHAPTER 13

The Angel Lesson

Jude Verse 9 (AMP): But when [even] the archangel Michael, contending with the devil, judicially argued (disputed) about the body of Moses, he dared not [presume to]bring an abusive condemnation against him, but [simply] said, The Lord rebuke you!

This is imperative that we get this. What we say is sooooo very important. At all times we should be paying attention to what is coming out of our mouths. The words we speak. Especially when we are in dispute with someone. In disagreement. In judicial argument.

As a reminder: the story behind the verse above is this; Moses basically did everything right but one. Remember, he was under the Old Covenant of Law and the blood of animals which did not take away the sins of the people, only pushed them off for a year. Moses obeyed God in all that God told him to do, except one little itty bitty thing. One tiny infraction that gave the devil the legal right to challenge. That tiny infraction was at the rock when God told Moses to speak to the rock to bring forth water so that the people of Israel, who were still in the desert after leaving Egypt, would not die from thirst. Moses spoke to the rock, but nothing happened right away. So Moses smote the rock and water came forth. But God did not tell him to hit the rock. So Moses was in disobedience, and because of this, he was not permitted to enter the Promise land. Satan thought that upon the death of Moses', because of this legal infraction, that he (Satan) had the right to the body of Moses. God dispatched the archangel Michael to put a legal stop to Satan's claim.

Now think about this. Here are two archangels. Satan, or Lucifer, was the highest archangel there was, second only to God, before he was cast out of Heaven. Michael is an archangel still in constant service to God. Michael could have told Satan off! God sent me and you are a liar and a thief Satan! You got yourself thrown out of Heaven! You lost your position! I am His archangel and I am here to retrieve the body of Moses per God's instructions! You low life you! You snake! Get your hands off of him!

But that is not how it went down. And correctly so. He, Michael, *dared not* to bring an <u>abusive</u> condemnation against him, Satan. He did not name call. He did not accuse in a shaking of the head, wagging and pointing of the finger, I am justified in what I am doing sort of way. He had RESPECT – yes, for Satan. For the fact that Satan was an archangel, second only to God at one time. Doesn't matter if he was thrown out of Heaven for his sin. Doesn't matter if he's a liar and a thief and the father of it. He is a creation of God's. Period.

Now I'm not saying we are supposed to go around giving respect to Satan and him minions. Leave archangels to deal with archangels. Their business is not our business when it comes to the business between them. Know your place! Plus, Satan and his minions are now locked up for the next 1,000 years so it is not our concern about him at all right now! It is how we speak to each other. It is how Christians speak to other Christians, first and foremost. And it is most especially how we speak to all people, including and especially to non-Christians. It doesn't matter how justified you may be, even legally so, in what the matter at hand may be. Keep a guard on your heart so that the words that proceed from your lips are respectful. Love. Kindness. Patience. Understanding that the person you are in direct opposition with is just as much a creature of God and is loved by God just as much as God loves you. God is no respecter of person. And frankly, God is a communist! Don't freak out, more on that at another writing. We must clean up what we say. Stop and think about it. Seriously, what would Jesus say in this situation? It doesn't matter how justified you are. How correct you are legally. How angry you are! Do NOT give into your flesh! Do not say just whatever you want because it makes you feel better in the moment! How would you want to be spoken to??? Would you want to be accused? Would you want to be called an idiot? Stupid? WRONG?

We have entered the Age of Shalom. If words create, and they do, how are we supposed to bring in the fullness of Shalom when we are still speaking words of self-justification. Name calling. Words that are the opposite of peace, joy, love, respect, patience, kindness, honor.

Get nitpicky with yourselves. You start monitoring every word that comes out of your mouth. I don't care if you have to do it 24/7 for the next 5 years. Monitor every word that comes out of your mouth in all situations that you face. Line your words up with the words of Jesus. Check what you say to line up with the Word of God. Get close with God so that He will give you the words you need in any given situation. That is what the Holy Spirit is for. It is time to grow up.

Words create. It is the Age of Shalom. Let's get our words lined up with Shalom.

CHAPTER 14

Belongs to Who?

Back in 1984 I was attending a church in Grass Valley, CA. My son was just a baby and one Sunday morning I was picking him up from the church nursery after services. Now I was wearing a pin, a broche that I got from Avon. It was a gold crescent moon with a couple of silver stars hanging from tiny chains below it. As I was picking up my son from nursery, a fellow parishioner had noticed the broche I was wearing. He came up and proceeded to tell me that he used to be a high priest in a Satanic cult years ago. They had signs and symbols that they used in their worship of Satan ceremonies. The crescent moon with stars beneath was one of the symbols they used.

Now, being the astute person that God made me, I could tell that he was trying to save me from Satanic symbols and was kindly indicating to me that I may not want to ever wear that broche again. I thanked him, got my son and left.

I went home and pondered that for a little while. True, God created all things, the heavens and the earth and all that is in them – the whole entire universe. True, God originally gave man dominion over all the earth. True, Adam gave away that dominion to Satan in the Garden of Eden. True, that immediately after Jesus was baptized by John in the River Jordan, he was taken out into the wilderness and tempted of Satan for 40 days. At that time, Satan had dominion, or "ownership," if you will, of the earth and all the things therein and he even told Jesus that he would give him the kingdoms of the earth if Jesus would bow down and worship him. And, at that time, Satan was perfectly within his rights to make that offer.

However, when Jesus was crucified, that ALL changed. Jesus took it back! Satan no longer had or has any ownership of anything, not heaven, not earth, not anything in them. He certainly does not own the moon and the stars.

So I said, out loud, "Satan, you don't own the moon and the stars. You don't own this broche. You don't get to use what is God's creation and pervert it for your purposes. I take back what you stole! I take it back in the name of Jesus!"

I still have the broche. I did not wear it again at that church, for that man's sake. But I do wear it when I want to.

Here's the point. Satan hasn't owned anything for the last 2,000 years. And now that he is off planet, he REALLY doesn't own anything! We are still allocating 'stuff' to him, afraid to learn things or take things or own things because we associate it with belonging to Satan. No, nothing belongs to the now absentee! It belongs to us through stewardship to God!

So let's go back to Stewardship 101. This time, take Satan completely out of the equation, because he IS completely out of the equation, and start taking care of ALL that is on the earth and the moon and the planet and the stars!

Let's clean up the mess he has left behind. Yep, and right now it is quite the mess left! But Hallelujah! The clean-up isn't going to be nearly as hard as we think because we do not have Satan and his minions constantly stirring up trouble!

Look, I realize this is going to take a little bit to really sink in. But Satan is not here! We have a 1,000 years without him! Start knowing this and thinking and walking and doing with the realization that he and his minions are nowhere to be seen, felt, heard. We are not dealing with him anymore. We are dealing with ourselves and with our neighbors.

And honesty, a 1,000 years ain't all that long. So it would behoove us to get this down pat by the time Satan is released again, for but a little while. We need to be ready. And we will be. I am quite confident about that. But none of us, in this time, need to be concerned about that. Now, we must learn to live in the Millennium. In Shalom. Which is right now! We are not still waiting for it. It is NOW.

ABOUT THE AUTHOR

Gina Welsh is a writer, artist, musician, accountant, and author. She lives with her husband and various pets in Duluth, Minnesota.